Dewey I THESS. 5. 16 TO 18

The sounds of the beach drifted into the houseboat and made Alec drowsy as he lay on the bunk trying to forget Miss Higgins. He yawned cavernously, like the sound of rushing wind, and relaxed into the mattress. Soon he fell into a slumber, with thoughts of Miss Higgins creeping back into his mind.

*You must go into a home—incapable of looking after yourself— not getting proper nourishment—just look at this filthy mess.*

He stirred uneasily and turned over onto his side, munching his jaws up and down in the habit of old people. He drifted into a deep sleep.

Phantom figures of old men shuffled down shiny corridors. His legs hurt as he stumbled along with them. Rimless glasses stared from vacant faces, wheelchairs creaked and groaned down a dark tunnel. Alec's heart pounded and his eyelids twitched as he felt himself falling into a gray, misty sea.

He moaned hoarsely and woke with a start, his pillow damp with sweat. He lay there for a few minutes, confused and lonely. Stiffly, he got up, closed the windows on the cold night air and realized he had forgotten to have his dinner.

# Chapter Two

Young Chris hurried out of his father's general store, carefully carrying the Crockpot of stew his mother had given him for Mr. Thomson.

He followed the little sandy track that led to the houseboat, the golden glow of the morning sunlight tinting his hair as it was blown about his face by the fresh sea breeze.

Watching him were two pairs of eyes peering out of the houseboat window. One pair belonged to old Alec, the other pair, which were button bright and brown, to Ben. Suddenly, a little ball of black and white energy burst through the open hatch and, scarcely touching the deck, shot into the air, landing on all fours on the grassy bank. He jumped up at Chris and nearly knocked the Crockpot out of his hands.

"Hullo, Ben boy, how are you? Careful now, oh good dog, sit now, sit. Quick, Mr. Thomson," said Chris as Ben danced uncontrollably around him, "take the stew or I'll drop it. Ben's just too excited!"

Chris passed the Crockpot through the open window to Alec, who carefully put it on the table next to him. "My word, your mum is good to me. Come along in. I feel like some good company today—cheer me up a bit."

Chris climbed the ladder onto the deck, ran below and squatted on the bottom step, his sandy brown feet resting on a piece of tattered linoleum. Ben's nails clicked on the steps as he danced down and jumped up on the chair near the table.

"How are you, Mr. Thomson? Have you taught Ben any new tricks?"

"Well, haven't felt like tricks lately. Had a lot on me mind, but he's a smart dog—aren't ya, lad." Ben wriggled all over with pleasure, nearly falling off the chair with excitement. "Off you go now. I'll take you for a bit of a walk later, though you've been a bad boy lately."

"I'll take him later on, Mr. Thomson," interrupted Chris, "but can we work on the model boat now?" He looked around the houseboat. "Gee, wish I had a real boat like this. I'd live in it all by myself, just like you!"

"Yeah, a man couldn't wish for anything better. It's a great life on a boat," Alec replied, looking proudly around him. "That Higgins woman is tryin' to put me in a home and take me boat," he muttered. "I tell you, I won't have it, I won't be ordered about." He jumped up and thumped the kitchen table. "Fester and tarnation! I just won't have it!" he said through the clacking of his false teeth.

Chris watched in fascination. "Please, Mr. Thomson, can we work on the model boat now?"

Alec looked at him sharply, then smiled. "Yes, of course, lad, go and get it off the cupboard, but be careful with it. Very nearly had it smashed yesterday, with that woman poking around."

Chris went over to the cupboard in the corner of the kitchen and lifted down a partly finished boat, made entirely of matchsticks. He carefully placed it on the table. "Boy, I can hardly wait till it's finished! Can I really keep it, Mr. Thomson?"

"Yes, of course you can, not much use to me. I've got one of me own—a real one," he added, chuckling. "Get the book now with the picture of the *Cutty Sark;* then you can start cuttin' the burnt ends off the matches. Now, let's have a look at it. Mmm, you'll want to cut about thirty matches, about this long." He cut one for Chris. "Looks like the cabin should go on next. Be careful of your fingers or your dad will be cross with me!"

They worked silently for a while as Chris cut the matches and handed them to Alec.

"Gee," said Chris, "wouldn't it be great to really sail a boat like the *Cutty Sark*. Would your houseboat sail, Mr. Thomson?"

20

Alec was gluing some pieces together. "Well, guess there's no reason why it shouldn't, no reason at all. Thing did float once," he muttered.

"If I had it, I'd sail it up the Barrier Reef. Do you reckon it would go that far?" asked Chris, cutting sharp points on some matches and handing them to Alec, who was fitting them onto the cabin.

"Nice up there," Alec answered thoughtfully. "Islands everywhere—a man could really get away from it all, be a real beachcomber. Palm trees, coconuts, a tropical paradise. No welfare department near those little islands. I wonder . . ." His eyes lit up and he looked at Chris. "The Barrier Reef, yes, of course, that's it— the Barrier Reef. You've got it, lad!" he shouted. "You've hit on a wonderful idea. It's amazing!"

He jumped up, almost knocking over the table. "Why on earth didn't I think of this before—must be getting old and silly. Huh, I'll fix that awful welfare woman and the authorities. I'll show 'em all," he snorted. "Old folks home indeed!" He went off into the bedroom, bent down under the bunk and pulled out the old suitcase. Ben was taken by surprise and scrambled for safety into another corner.

Alec's trembling hands fumbled at the rusty catches and finally managed to open the suitcase, revealing the contents—a pair of binoculars, an assortment of old clothes, photographs curled and brown with age.

"That's it, that's what I was looking for," he laughed and pulled out a large and beautifully detailed map of the Queensland coastline. "This was given to me by a mate of mine during the Second World War," he said excitedly. "It's an aerial-view map used by the army. See, it's got every little inlet and hill marked. Looks real, doesn't it?"

"Boy, it sure is a good map, Mr. Thomson. Look at all the islands! Gee, I'd love to go. Can I go? It's my vacation soon. I want to go on a real adventure. Boy, we couldn't get lost with a map like that," reasoned Chris.

Alec chuckled, completely carried away, "Well, you're small enough for a cabin boy, but, er, don't think your dad would like the idea much." Getting up from the table, he said, "Leave that matchstick model, my lad. We're going over to the shop to tell your dad all about this, right now!"

"Oh boy, is he going to be excited," said Chris, jumping up and down. "Come here, Ben, we're going to sea!" Grabbing Ben under his arm, he hopped and danced about the kitchen, nearly knocking Alec's walking stick from under him.

"Easy on, lad, nearly had me over," said Alec, laughing. Then he scuttled, sideways like an old crab, up the stairs and onto the deck, down the ladder, and was almost halfway along the track before Chris and Ben caught up with him.

Alec barged into Gerry's shop. "Gerry, Gerry," he shouted, upsetting a magazine rack. "Where the dickens are ya."

"What on earth's the matter, Alec," said Gerry, running from the kitchen.

Alec wobbled on his stick, hardly able to speak for puffing and blowing, cheeks aflame and white eyebrows riding up and down like crested waves. His mouth opened and shut soundlessly like that of a goldfish.

"For goodness sake, Alec, if you don't sit down you'll have a heart attack," said Gerry with alarm.

"Don't need to sit down. I'm all right, I tell ya, I never felt better," shouted Alec. "They won't get the chance to condemn me boat and put me in a home, 'cos I won't be here."

"Where will you be?" asked Gerry impatiently.

"I'm going to sail the houseboat up the Barrier Reef." And before Gerry could answer, Alec added, "Can't stay talking to you all day, must get back and start preparing to refloat the boat. I'll be leaving in May!" Shrieking with laughter, he rushed out of the shop.

"Mary," Gerry yelled to his wife, "stop what you're doing and listen to this. Alec Thomson's just been in—"

"Yes, I thought I heard his voice. He sounded upset. He's all right, isn't he?"

"I'm not so sure, Mary. Do you know what he's going to do? He thinks he can refloat the houseboat and sail it up the Barrier Reef. It would sink in a duck pond! He's as mad as a hatter. That welfare woman is quite right. He ought to be put in a home!"

"Dad," said Chris excitedly, "Mr. Thomson said I could go too— as a cabin boy. I won't have to go to that stupid camp. Just wait till I tell the kids at school!"

"You'll be waiting, all right," said his father in amazement.

"Please, Dad, it was my idea. It'll be really great. We could be in all the newspapers!"

"I don't believe it, I just don't believe it."

"Now, dear," Mary said. "Don't carry on so. We will all discuss it later. I'm sure Mr. Thomson will come to his senses eventually."

24    "Can't be too soon," said Gerry. "He's as nutty as a fruit cake!"

Danley. PROV. 8-29

# Chapter Three

Alec lay on his bunk after the best night's sleep he had had in years. The warm morning sun filtered through his partly opened blind, making the old bedroom glow with color and warmth.

He was quietly thinking of the journey ahead—the open sea, beautiful tropical islands and the rainforests of North Queensland. Oh yes, he smiled, I'll be a real beachcomber. No welfare departments to bother me there. Just me and Ben. I can hardly wait! And, laughing to himself, he thought: That Higgins woman told me I have to be out on the first of May. Huh, I'll be out all right. I'll be sailing off right under her nose!

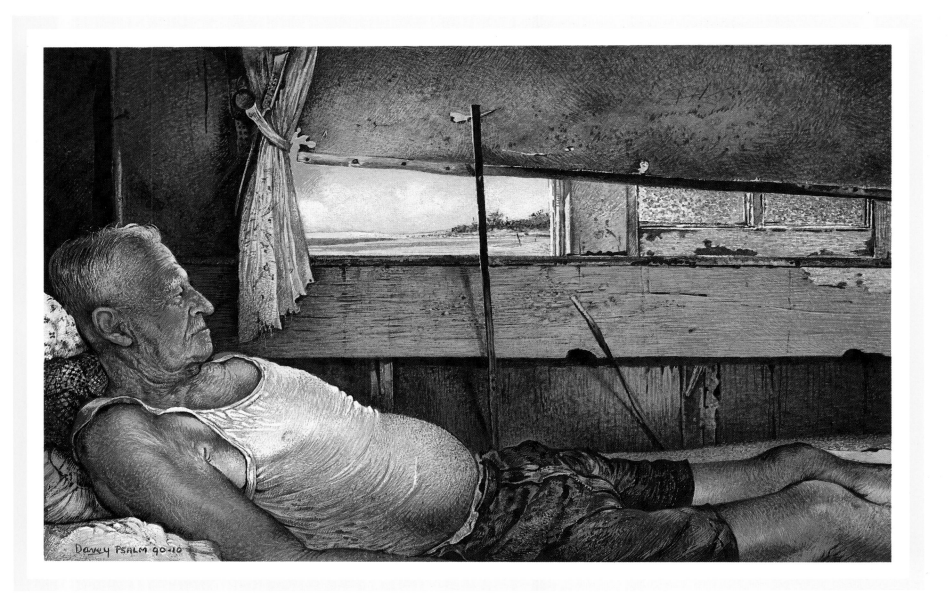

Later Alec leaned on the rail of the boat and watched the pelicans soar overhead in the clear sunlight. He liked this time of day best, when everything in the passage was busy with activity. He watched the gulls below the boat as they ran in and out of the receding tide looking for morsels of food, then listened to the voices of fishermen calling from their dinghies and heard the laughter of children carried on the wind.

"Come on, boy," he said to Ben, "let's start our tour of inspection," and promptly stubbed his foot against a loose plank on the deck. "Drat that plank. I'll have to fix it soon as possible, could fall on that in a rough sea. Stay there, Ben, I'm going up to check the roof."

Climbing on a pineapple crate, he managed to haul himself up onto the roof. The wind whipped away at his roomy shorts, which flapped against his legs, making him look like a big old elephant.

He tapped and prodded at the partly rotted surface and thought to himself: Probably just a bit of patching here and there will do, hasn't leaked much since Gerry tarred it last year. Yes, looks pretty good, considering the salt air is on it all the time.

Ben was nervously fidgeting about on the deck when Alec clambered down, breathing hard after all the exertion.

"What's the matter, boy? You look worried; you'll be all right, you'll love it up North. Come on, we're going to check below now."

Ben was uneasy but he followed his master down the steps to the kitchen. He sensed something was different, something was going to happen. His master usually just lay about on his bunk all day.

"Now that really does need fixing," said Alec, contemplating a large gaping hole under the stairway. He gave the surrounding metal a poke with his stick and it crumbled tiredly onto the floor.

Ben peered in, nose twitching, ears pricked. "Stop sniffin' about, Ben. Nothing in there 'cept me old crab pots. Come on, let's have a cuppa tea. We've missed our lunch today and I'm feeling a bit hungry."

Ben gave a woof of agreement.

28

Alec made a pot of tea and cut two rounds of bread, spreading them thickly with butter and plum jam. He propped a newspaper up on a carton of milk and settled down to a cup of tea and yesterday's news.

The late afternoon was darker than usual. The sun hung above the Maleny Ranges, but a specter-like mass of black cloud moved very slowly across the evening sky toward the ocean. The failing light had an eerie luminous glow, making the island appear dark, with one dead tree etched against the skyline.

Alec went over to the cupboard and found an old envelope and busily started writing on the back—

THINGS I MUST DO TOMORROW
1. Fix plank
2. Patch roof
3. See Gerry about big hole
4. Paint the cabin (not necessarily tomorrow)

PROVISIONS TO TAKE ON JOURNEY
1. Big bag potatoes
2. Big bag onions
3. 50 cans baked beans
4. 50 cans dog food

He had almost run out of space and was about to continue on an old paper bag when the back hatch started to rattle and bang.

"Tarnation. Wind's blowing up again." He went down to the end of the boat to close it and craned his neck out to look up at the sky. "Great Nelly! That's a black cloud. Think I'd better batten me boat. We'll get a bit of rain tonight." And he hurried round to secure all the windows, leaving only the front hatch open for Ben to get in and out.

Davey 2 SAM. 22.12

He'd finished all of Mary's stew and was too excited to bother about cooking, so he got out the last tin of baked beans and ate them straight from the can. He gave Ben his dog food, then got back to the list and the map of the Queensland coastline.

"Now, let me see." He moved his stubby pencil along the map. "Yes, I'll stick pretty close to the coast and head straight for the islands. Mm—there's Keppel Island, near Rockhampton." He moved his pencil on and stopped suddenly at Hayman Island. "That's it, that's where I'll go. All the rich tourists go there. I can hire me boat out for fishing trips and make a lot of money. I won't even need the blinkin' pension."

"Great Nelly, I'm all nervous and excited," he muttered. "Think I'll have to have something to settle me down." Going to the cupboard he took out a bottle of rum that Gerry had given him the week before, on his eighty-second birthday. He poured out a large tumblerful and downed it in one long gulp. He coughed and spluttered. "Boy, that was good. Reckon I could sail around the world now," he chortled.

He took his map and list into the bedroom and lay down to think. The rum made him drowsy and within five minutes he was fast asleep, mouth wide open and snoring loudly, with the map draped across his stomach.

# Chapter Four

Ben crawled out from underneath the bunk, observed his master flat on his back snorting and snoring, stood for a moment watching him closely, then pressed his cold wet muzzle on Alec's mouth. His master muttered something in his sleep, then turned over on his side and continued to snore even louder.

Ben scratched at a flea for a minute, then trotted out into the kitchen to check his food bowl. A minute particle had lodged against the side. He was trying to lick at it when his attention was distracted by a dog barking somewhere in the park along the foreshore. Sensing the urgency of the call, he ran up onto the deck and stood "pointing," nose twitching, tail vibrating.

The wind blew fiercely, as if trying to peel the black and white coat from the little dog's back. Excitement surged through him. He jumped from the deck and ran off to join a brown dog chasing the wind through the park. They raced together, biting playfully at each other and snapping at papers flying confetti-like in whirling eddies. The trees were alive with motion, sending birds fluttering into the sky. Ben was completely carried away by the strange madness of the wind, running about in a frenzy of joy. Suddenly, something fell on top of him, tangling itself around his legs, pinning him to the ground. He tore frantically at the net, aware that the brown dog had been caught up with him. Clawing, snarling and yapping, the two dogs were thrown into a loud howling mass of dogs. Two wire doors clanged and snapped shut.

"Got that little foxy fellow. Got his mate too," said a ginger-haired man. "Come on, we'll get this lot back to the pound. Looks like that storm's coming our way."

George and Sid always liked doing the beach run but today had not gone well. They'd had a flat tire up near Moffat Beach and then Sid was bitten by a white poodle.

"Mind you," said George, "it was your own stupid fault. You never should trust any of the critters. Never did like blinkin' poodles."

"It's blowin' up real bad," said Sid. "Maybe we could sit it out in the pub until it blows over." He added hopefully, "Anyway, I feel a bit thirsty and we could have a game of darts."

"Nuh. Heard something on the radio about a freak storm and king tides tonight, better get back. Listen to those yappers back there," said George, who was trying hard to keep the truck from skidding about. "Boy, that big gust nearly blew us across the other side! Can't see a thing in this rain."

Just then a large limb flew off a huge gum tree and crashed across their windscreen, showering them with milky-white glass. George tried desperately to keep the truck on the road. Unable to see, he went into a side skid and headed straight into a ditch already filling with water.

Pandemonium broke out in the back as the door burst open and the dogs hurtled about, falling on top of each other, snarling and biting. The brown dog was almost dead, blood oozing from his mouth. A mud-splattered white poodle cried pitifully in the corner as Ben snarled at the large bull terrier sprawled on top of him.

36

Slowly and painfully the dogs scrambled toward the door and tumbled out into the storm. The blackness enveloped them. Ben watched the other dogs peel off in all directions, but the brown dog looked dazed and just stood there, head low, staring listlessly. In the distance dogs were barking and the men called to one another, their voices trailing off into the night with the shriek of the wind.

Ben looked anxiously at the brown dog for some seconds, then turned and scampered off. He couldn't see in the blackness and blinding rain, but his dog sense told him which was the right direction.

Head down, he started back along the main road, gripping firmly with his strong claws so as not to be blown off his feet. Caloundra was very near but totally blacked out by the storm. He limped slowly along, making his way to the turnoff leading to Golden Beach.

Knowing he was very close, he tried to hurry. The wind buffeted him about, sometimes rolling him over and over. He had almost reached the park in front of Gerry's shop when he saw the water.

Fearfully he started to paddle through it. It gurgled and hissed at him, foaming across his body as he partly waded and partly swam along toward the track which led to the boat.

Danby  Psalm 104:3

# Chapter Five

The tattered curtains on the houseboat rustled uneasily from their rusted rods as the rain tried to force its way through the gaps under the sills. Already it was blasting its way down through the front hatch. Alec was still flat out on his bunk, snoring.

The wind began to roar now, vibrating the boat violently, and waves across the passage reared into an angry churning mass of foam. The tide was rising and sheets of rain pelted down. The she-oaks screamed as if in pain as branches were ripped off and hurtled missile-like through the air. Foam sailed high on the wind across to the houses beyond the foreshore.

Alec's bedroom window, unable to withstand the onslaught any longer, gave in with a splintering crash, sending glass and water flying right across his bunk. Waking with a howl of terror and pain, he rolled off the bunk and on to the floor, screaming, "Ah, ah, help!"

Terrified, he lay there with blood trickling from a small cut on his cheek. Slowly coming to his senses in the flooding cabin, he dragged himself up and felt around for the torch which he always kept near by.

"Thundering Nelly," he yelled. "It must be a cyclone!" Remembering Ben, he crawled wildly about. "Ben, Ben," he called. "Where are ya', boy? Oh, poor lad must have run off into the storm."

He found his stick, waded ankle deep to the front steps and onto the deck, and for the first time felt the full force of the wind. "Ben," he called, his voice falling flat against the storm. Ben must be sheltering somewhere, he thought frantically.

Staggering blindly in the rain and using his stick for support, he managed to make it to the outside ladder and put his full weight on the top step. His foot shot out from under him on the slippery surface and he slid straight down the ladder, hitting his head as he went.

Alec was in a half-sitting position, his head and shoulders resting on the ladder, the bulk of his body on the ground now being covered by the rising water. Here Ben, floundering and splashing through the blackness, saw his master—the old man he loved. He was delirious with joy and barked and howled, jumping about Alec's body. But his master didn't move. He looked anxiously into the cold white face and saw blood oozing from a cut. Terror seized him and he started to run off, but he turned and came back. Whining loudly, he lay down, his little rump partly submerged in saltwater, paws resting on Alec's chest.

The walking stick floated near by and bumped gently against Ben. He made a tired grab at it, missed and howled piteously into the night. It bumped against him again. This time he made a determined grab and gripped it firmly between his strong teeth.

41

Then he struggled to his feet and splashed off along the track to Gerry's shop.

From the side porch he could hear people talking and saw the woman holding a blanket across a broken window. He scratched desperately at the door, dropped the stick with a clatter onto the wooden veranda and slid away into the darkness.

The voices stopped for a moment as Gerry opened the door to investigate. "Why, that's Alec Thomson's walking stick."

Completely exhausted, Ben crawled up against a tree trunk, and lay there quivering and panting. His instinct told him he must get back to his master. But he felt himself slipping away into a hazy coma. He didn't hear the Land-Rover drive past him, and he didn't see the body of his master being gently lifted into the back.

Just before dawn, Ben came out of his mist-shrouded dream and slowly rose to his feet. He dragged himself down the sandy track toward home and back to his master. He moved a little faster when he saw the houseboat ahead. The hatches had been ripped off by the wind and tossed into the heaving sea; the roof lay splintered all about the boat and ugly gaping holes grinned death-like through the broken sides of the cabin. The tide was receding slowly, leaving the boat full of foaming water. Ben crawled up onto the deck, whining softly. There was no greeting, no familiar voice or sign of his master, but it was home. If he could only get under the bunk, he'd be safe.

He took tottering little steps across the deck, skidding about on the wet, oily surface. His eyes filled with stinging salt and were partly closed. From habit he took a little jump onto the first wooden step but sank swiftly into the black seawater as it surged backward and forward. The mass of dirty foam caught the helpless little body, dragging it downward. Choking and gasping and clawing at nothing, he tried desperately to keep his small black nose above the water.
Frantically, he surfaced only to sink back again with exhaustion.

# Chapter Six

Gerry, Mary and Chris were up at first light to inspect the damage to their shop and the houseboat. They walked across the park. Three caravans were lying splintered on their sides near the bend in the road. Several large trees had been uprooted and branches were strewn over the ground.

"That's the worst storm we've ever been through," said Gerry. "I hadn't realized it was this bad."

"Poor Mr. Thomson, thank God he is going to be all right," said Mary.

"Yes, he's a tough old bloke. Just a few cuts, bad knock on the head and shock. Would have killed me," he said dryly.

"Mum, Miss Higgins isn't going to put him into a home, is she?" asked Chris anxiously.

"Well, dear, your father and I discussed it all night. We have decided to let Mr. Thomson have the spare room."

"Oh gee, Mum, Dad, that's great. And as soon as he's feeling better, we can start another model ship."

Davey GEN. I·A.

Their first sight of the houseboat was as a jagged outline against the pale morning sky, with the flagpole leaning at an angle and the iron railing twisted and bent.

They cautiously picked their way toward it over the broken deck and stood peering down into the hull filled with murky, sluggish water. Pieces of wood and smashed chairs floated about and a partly submerged mattress, spread with a sodden map and tattered curtains, lay against a wall. A brass basin, badly bent, bobbed up and down with the pots and saucepans.

Chris leaned down from the top step to pick up a broken pole and used it to poke about in the water. "Don't think there's much in here worth worrying about, Dad." He peered through toward the end of the boat into the bedroom. "Looks like a suitcase back there in the bedroom."

"You better get that," said his father.

Chris lowered himself into the water and waded waist-deep toward the suitcase. Reaching the bunk, he stretched out his hand to pull the case from the shadows and there, lying on top, covered in brine, was a small, shivering, black and white dog.

Davey  Ecc. 11-7

Chris's heart missed a beat. As he placed his hand on the little dog, Ben's eyes flickered and opened.

"Dad," cried Chris in astonishment. "It's Ben here. It's Ben!" Tears in his eyes, he very gently took Ben into his arms.

Ben whimpered slightly and nestled against Chris's warm body. His coat was caked in salt but he just managed to wag his tail. Chris carefully carried him up through the hatch and into the brilliant sunshine.

They stood on the deck, stroking and talking to him.

"Poor little fellow, Dad. He must have been here all the time."

"Yes," said Gerry, looking at the boat. "It's a miracle he survived. If only he could talk. Then he might be able to explain how on earth that walking stick got on our porch—I wonder."

At the word "stick" Ben opened his sad brown eyes and whimpered.